What on Earth?
Hurricanes

What on Earth?

Can a hurricane do any good?

Turn this page to find out!

First published in 2005 by
Book House an imprint of
The Salariya Book Company
25 Marlborough Place
Brighton
BN1 1UB

Please visit The Salariya Book Company at: **www.salariya.com**

HB ISBN 1-905087-33-0
PB ISBN 1-905087-34-9

Visit our website at **www.book-house.co.uk**
for free electronic versions of:
You Wouldn't Want to be an Egyptian Mummy!
You Wouldn't Want to be a Roman Gladiator!
Avoid joining Shackleton's Polar Expedition!
You Wouldn't Want to Sail on a 19th-Century Whaling Ship!

Due to the changing nature of internet links, The Salariya Book Company has
developed an online list of websites related to the subject of this book.
This site is updated regularly. Please use this link to access the list:
http://www.book-house.co.uk/WOE/hurricanes

A catalogue record for this book is available
from the British Library.

Printed and bound in China.

Editors: Ronald Coleman
                          Sophie Izod
Senior Art Editor: Carolyn Franklin
DTP Designer: Mark Williams

Picture Credits Julian Baker & Janet Baker (J B
Illustrations): 6-7, 8, 9(t), Nick Hewetson: 3, 10-11, 18, 20-
21, Corbis: 1, 13, 16, 17, 24-25, 28, Digital Vision: 14-15,
19, 23, 26, 29, Douglas R Clifford/St. Petersburg
Times/Florida: 9(b), NASA Langley Research Center: 30-31,
NASDA/NASA/JPL: 15

Cover credits: Corbis

What on Earth?

Yes!

Hurricanes cause water
surges which spread coral
eggs and help more coral
to grow.

What on Earth?
Hurricanes

CATHERINE CHAMBERS

What do satellites have to do with hurricanes?

Turn to page 11 to find out!

BOOK HOUSE

Contents

What on Earth?

Hurricane Floyd

In 1999 Hurricane Floyd brought so much rain to the United States that thirteen states declared themselves disaster zones.

Introduction

A hurricane is a violent tropical storm that forms over an ocean. It is a **whirling spiral** of wind that thunders across Earth's surface at speeds of more than 119 kilometres (74 miles) per hour.

How strong is a hurricane?

A hurricane is no ordinary storm. Its winds can uproot massive trees, blow down bridges and easily rip the roofs from buildings. It brings with it driving rain and **crashing** thunderstorms. Its effect on the ocean can also bring great danger from the sea itself.

What's inside a hurricane?

The area at the centre of a hurricane is known as the 'eye' of the storm. It is surrounded by a whirling spiral of wind. When the 'eye' is **overhead**, the hurricane conditions come to a stop. The sky becomes blue again and for a short time, all is calm.

What is a hurricane?

The effects of a hurricane are felt in three separate stages. The first phase of a hurricane brings raging winds, torrents of rain and fierce thunder and lightning. As the eye of the storm passes overhead, the sun shines and all seems calm again. But then the backlash of the storm sweeps in for another wave of destruction.

Huge circle of clouds around hurricane

Eye of the storm

Upward spiral of wind

Water vapour (water in the form of gas) in the rising air condenses to form thick clouds

Cool air flows out from the top
of the storm and forms a huge
circle of cloud

Warm, damp
air rises from
the sea

The spinning
motion of Earth
makes the
winds travel
upwards

Coastline

Winds of cool
air blow in

Rain falls
below

7

where do hurricanes happen?

Hurricanes only form over hot tropical oceans that lie either side of the equator. They spin furiously towards land and the Caribbean Islands, Central America and the east coast of the United States are most affected.

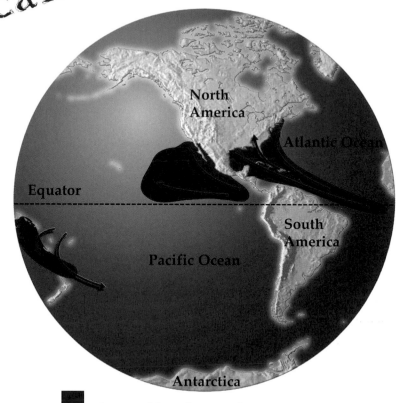

North America

Atlantic Ocean

Equator

South America

Pacific Ocean

Antarctica

Areas of hurricanes shown on maps

What a lot of wind!

In the northern hemisphere cyclones spin in an anti-clockwise direction and anticyclones in a clockwise direction. In the southern hemisphere it's the other way round.

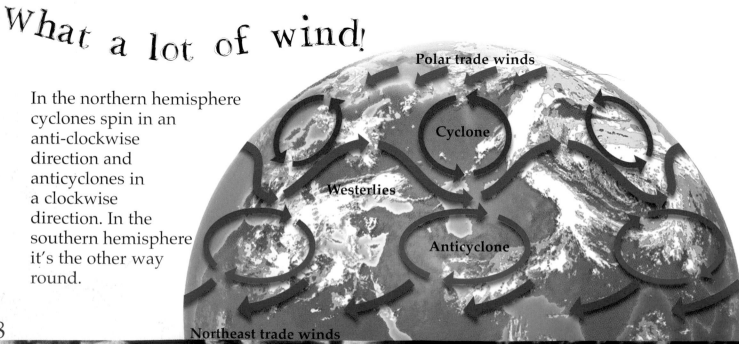

Polar trade winds

Cyclone

Westerlies

Anticyclone

Northeast trade winds

What is a typhoon?

Asia

Europe

Africa

Equator

Indian Ocean

Australia

Pacific Ocean

Antarctica

➡️ **Direction of hurricanes**

When hurricanes happen in the western Pacific and hit Japan and the Philippines, they're called '**typhoons**'. When they hit India and Australia they are called 'tropical **cyclones**'.

What are hurricane force winds?

Hurricane force winds are winds that blow at the same speed as hurricanes but do not develop into full hurricane conditions. They can be up to 119 kilometres (74 miles) per hour.

Hurricane Francis hitting the east coast of Florida

9

Can hurricanes be spotted?

Scientists can track the movement of hurricanes by watching satellite pictures. Satellite tracking has made it possible to issue **warnings** of a hurricane's likely path and ferocity. Aircraft fly into the eye of the storm to gather information about wind-speed, temperature and humidity levels inside a hurricane. The *Doppler* radar system plots the shape and speed of a hurricane.

Information is also collected by aircraft. In the US, special aircraft fly into hurricanes to monitor what is happening.

Balloons filled with helium gas are sent into the atmosphere, carrying instruments that measure air pressure, temperature and humidity.

How strong are hurricanes?

Hurricanes are measured by their strength and by the damage they cause. There are five levels of hurricane, Category Five being the strongest. The wind speed of a Category One hurricane is 119 to 53 kilometres (74 to 95 miles) per hour. Category Five reaches speeds of more than 249 kilometres (155 miles) per hour.

How do satellites help?

Two types of weather satellites hover 36,000 kilometres (22,000 miles) above Earth's surface gathering data that helps meteorologists to analyse storm clouds and keep a close watch on hurricanes.

Polar-orbiting satellites travel from North pole to South pole, collecting information about temperatures and photographing the entire surface of Earth, one section at a time.

Polar-orbiting satellite

Geostationary satellite

Geostationary satellites always stay above the same point on Earth's surface, photographing the changing cloud patterns below.

What on Earth?

How are hurricanes named?

Hurricanes are given male and female names alternately, and alphabetically. So, for example, Bob might be followed by Caroline.

What makes the wind blow?

Warm air rises and as it does, cold air rushes in to take its place. This movement of cold air is wind. The more warm air that rises – the more wind there will be to replace it. A hurricane is wind in one of its most extreme forms.

Why do hurricanes happen?

Hurricanes occur in tropical oceans close to the equator, the hottest part of the world. Wind builds up across the oceans there, picking up moisture (water vapour) as it goes. As warm, moist air rises, it forms clouds and thunderstorms. The Earth's rotation (or spin) causes these storm winds to spiral into a hurricane.

When do hurricanes happen?

The hurricane season usually begins in June and ends in November – the hottest months in the tropics. Most hurricanes happen then, but some can happen earlier or later in the year. Climate changes may be affecting this pattern.

Satellite image of storm clouds gathering over North America

What on Earth?

Which direction?

This hurricane over North America will spin anti-clockwise because the wind flowing into it is pulling it to the right. This is called the Coriolis force.

Why are hurricanes seasonal?

It takes warm water and moist air to create a hurricane. Warm air picks up more moisture from the sea than cold air. So in summer a greater amount of warm, moist air rises from the oceans than at any other time of the year. Gusts of cold air (or wind) quickly sweep in. Hurricane winds that form in the middle of an ocean are much stronger than normal land winds.

What is a tornado?

When a hurricane reaches land, a tornado can form inside it. A tornado is a twisting column of spinning air that reaches down from a storm cloud to the ground. It can suck up anything in its path.

How fast is the wind speed of a hurricane?

Scientists use satellite images (left) to find out how fast winds are blowing. Hurricanes are shown in orange. When a tropical storm's winds hit 119 kilometres (74 miles) per hour it officially becomes a hurricane.

Ice

Land

Land

Land

How long do hurricanes last?

A hurricane's path can cover a long distance and may take days to reach land. Even then a hurricane can keep going, and most last several days.

What on Earth?

Fast, faster, fastest!

The fastest recorded wind speed in a hurricane was 512 kilometres (318 miles) per hour, and struck New York, New England and Canada in 1938.

Do hurricanes slow down?

Hurricanes are formed by the warm, moist air over an ocean. The wind speed of a hurricane rises swiftly as it approaches land but once there, it dies out as it gradually runs out of moisture.

Can hurricanes get stronger?

When a hurricane hits the Caribbean Islands, it picks up more moisture from the sea between each island which makes it even stronger by the time it reaches the coast of the USA.

What on Earth?

Not all bad?

Hurricanes move hot air away from the tropics. They help balance heat and moisture around the world. Without them large areas of the world would be too hot for animal or human life.

God of Storms?

The word hurricane comes from the Spanish word *huracan*, which probably came from the name of the Mayan storm god, 'Hunraken'.

What is a storm surge?

A storm surge can be deadly. It is a huge wave of seawater that can engulf the coast when a hurricane hits land. Hurricanes create **sudden** changes in air pressure which can cause sea levels to rise and waves to crash inland in a mighty storm surge.

Where do storm surges happen?

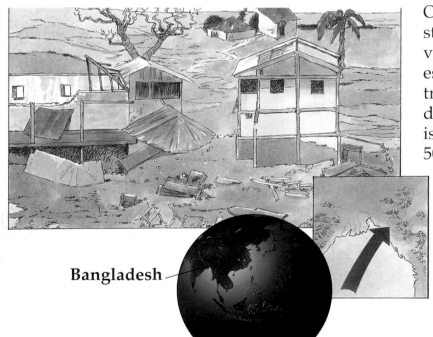

Bangladesh

One of the areas worst affected by storm surges is Bangladesh. It is very low-lying and has wide river estuaries. Huge storm surges travel far inland causing great destruction, especially when there is a high tide. In 1970 around 500,000 people died when a tropical cyclone hit this area.

The map (left) shows the direction from which the storm surges hit Bangladesh.

What on Earth?

How
high?

The highest storm surge ever recorded was in Bathurst Bay, Australia in 1899. The sea level rose by 13 metres (43 feet).

How much damage can they cause?

In August 2005, Hurricane Katrina caused a storm surge which affected a coastline 2,034 km (1,264 miles) long. The huge flow of water led to floods up to 7 metres (25 feet) deep in the city of New Orleans and many towns were completely destroyed across three states of the USA.

What's the damage?

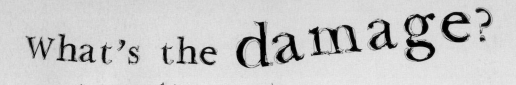

Hurricanes are extremely destructive, killing and injuring many people, and destroying homes and buildings. Crops are destroyed and power and water supplies, roads, bridges and rail networks are **torn apart**. There can be widespread flood damage too.

What's the cost?

The cost of cleaning up and starting again after a hurricane is enormous. It can take years to add up the true damage and costs caused by a hurricane.

Boats swept inland by a storm surge add to the chaos after a storm.

What on Earth?

Which hurricane caused the most damage?

Hurricane Katrina in 2005 is thought to be the most expensive hurricane ever – costing even more than the 25 billion dollars worth of damage caused by Hurricane Andrew in 1992.

How does wildlife cope?

Many animals sense that a storm is coming and head inland for safety. But the natural cycle of life for many birds, animals and insects is disrupted by a hurricane. Many animals die because their habitat is destroyed and their food source is wiped out.

How do creatures survive?

Some bird species now weave round-shaped nests that are less likely to be blown about by the wind. Others build their nests close to the ground.

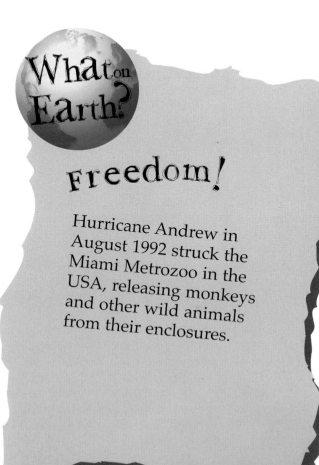

What on Earth?

Freedom!

Hurricane Andrew in August 1992 struck the Miami Metrozoo in the USA, releasing monkeys and other wild animals from their enclosures.

Trees uprooted by a hurricane can be replaced by planting young trees. However it will take a very long time for them to grow as big.

23

Are hurricanes getting worse?

Are hurricanes getting fiercer and more frequent or can scientists just detect and monitor them better now? *El Niño* and *La Niña* are sudden changes in wind direction and ocean currents that can affect the weather. It is thought that *El Niño* and *La Niña* affect the strength and frequency of hurricanes.

What is the Ozone hole?

Ozone is a kind of oxygen that forms a protective layer in the atmosphere high above the earth's surface. It absorbs the ultraviolet rays from the sun that would otherwise kill all living things. Worldwide pollution is destroying parts of the ozone layer and holes now exist over Antarctica and the Arctic. Worldwide, countries must take action now to stop this destruction getting worse.

This satellite photograph (right) shows the path of Hurricane Andrew in 1992.

What on Earth?

Desperation!

In 1998 during Hurricane Mitch, many parents in Honduras tied their children to the branches of tall trees to keep them from being swept away by the sea.

Can we avoid hurricanes?

A hurricane cannot be stopped, but with enough warning people can get out of its path. Countries that are most affected have 24 hour **warning** systems with frequent updates until the hurricane hits land. Meteorologists at national weather centres are linked to national radio and television networks and can post warnings on the internet. Forecasting is not easy though, because a hurricane's path and wind-speed can quickly change making them unpredictable.

Does anything else help?

New building regulations in countries like Jamaica and Australia aim to make structures safer. In the Caribbean Islands, the government is trying to develop special, shorter varieties of crops which can survive hurricane force winds.

How would **you** survive a **hurricane?**

If you live in an area that is prone to hurricanes, listen to all radio and television weather reports and advice. Warnings are helpful, but only when people act wisely. If an evacuation is ordered, leave as soon as possible. Follow these simple steps to overcome the danger of a hurricane.

Hurricane Dangers

Storm surge Most people are killed by flooding during a hurricane. Follow hurricane warnings and evacuate as soon as possible.

Flying debris can kill. Doors, roofs and chimneys will be ripped from buildings, avoid built-up areas.

Tornadoes Do not stay in your car as a very powerful tornado can carry a car for a distance of about one kilometre (half a mile).

Travel networks will be in chaos, roads may be washed away and bridges destroyed.

What to have Check-list

Be sure to wear **sturdy shoes**, you may have to travel a long way in difficult conditions. Make sure you have **tins of food** and a **tin opener**, as the hurricane may last for days. Take all **pets** indoors. Use **plywood** to board up windows to prevent breakage. A **generator** will supply you with electricity. A battery operated **radio** and spare **batteries** to listen to updates on the hurricane. **Money** as cash machines will stop working and a supply of **water** as running water may stop.

Hurricane facts

Huge hurricane waves called storm surges can reach 7 metres (20 feet)! They destroy birds, nesting sites and kill thousands of fish.

Hurricane winds can rage for nine or more days across the ocean and on land.

The 'eye' can be 32 kilometres (20 miles) wide from cloud wall to cloud wall!

In 1998, When Hurricane Georges hit islands in the Caribbean and the United States, twenty-eight tornadoes ran along with it.

In 2004, four hurricanes landed on the coast of Florida in just six weeks!

Hurricane Katrina, a Category Five storm, struck the Gulf coast of the United States on August 29th, 2005, causing massive devastation. Several towns and cities were evacuated and thousands of lives lost. It also caused the largest storm surge ever recorded on the east coast of America – up to 9 metres (30 feet) high.

Glossary

Air pressure The pushing down of air weighing down on a place.

Coriolis force The name of the effect that makes hurricanes spin in different directions depending on where they happen in the world.

Cyclone The name used for a hurricane in the southwest Pacific and Indian Oceans.

Equator Imaginary line around Earth's widest part.

Habitat The natural home of a plant or animal.

Humidity Warm, damp air.

Hurricane A vast spinning storm with winds over 119 kilometres (74 miles) per hour.

Northern hemisphere The top half of Earth.

Meteorologist A scientist who studies the weather.

Satellite A space technology system that orbits a planet recording information.

Tropics Hot regions that lie north and south of the equator.

Typhoon The name used for a hurricane in the China Seas.

Water vapour An invisible gas made up of tiny droplets of water in the air.

What do you **know** about hurricanes?

1 What is a hurricane's 'eye'?

2 Is there a hurricane season?

3 Which hurricane caused most damage?

4 What is a cyclone?

5 Do hurricanes have names?

6 Why do hurricanes end?

7 What is a storm surge?

8 What creates a hurricane?

9 Is El Niño a hurricane?

10 Where do hurricanes form?

Can you guess what *is* **different** about this **plane?**

Go to page 32 for the answer!

Index

Pictures are shown in **bold**.

Answers

1 The calm area at the centre of a hurricane. (See page 5)
2 Yes! June to November. (See page 12)
3 To date, Hurricane Andrew in 1992, but the final cost of Katrina in 2005 is still unknown and expected to be higher. (See page 21)
4 Another name for a hurricane. (See page 9)
5 Yes. (See page 11)
6 They run out of moisture. (See page 16)
7 A wall of seawater that crashes inland. (See page 18)
8 Warm, moist air. (See page 14)
9 No. (See page 24)
10 In warm tropical oceans around the equator. (See page 8)

This plane can fly very **high**. It carries special equipment to measure and record the **strength** and direction of the wind.

LOCH PRIMARY SCHOOL